THE INTENTIONAL DRIVE

J.J. TAYLOR

NEWMAN SPRINGS PUBLISHING
320 Broad Street
Red Bank, NJ 07701

First originally published by Newman Springs Publishing 2023

ISBN 979-8-89061-010-2 (Paperback)
ISBN 979-8-89061-011-9 (Digital)

Printed in the United States of America

Chapter 1

DREAMS

Dreams: (1) a series of thoughts, images, and sensations occurring in a person's mind during sleep; (2) a cherished aspiration, ambition, or ideal.

Dreams are self-explanatory; they are the visions we see mostly in our night. However, there are those in which we envision throughout our day. These are daydreams, the visions we have of being elsewhere when we are stuck where we do not want to be.

Dreams are an inspiring notion; they are the hopes we keep in our hearts, the vision we hold in our minds, and the ache we have in our souls as we go about our lives.

For most people, their dream is *just to survive another day*, while others dream of success or just to be happy.

Then there are those of us who *dare to dream bigger dreams*. It's more than just survival or success; it is the desire to live with a sense of purpose to be something greater.

Our dreams become the lifestyle we crave to be in, the lifestyle we choose to live every day. These are the dreams that would scare the pants off those in "survival mode" of life.

For those of us who *dare to dream bigger dreams*, those dreams become the heart light we follow; they become the value that creates the hustle in our hearts to better our future.

We know and understand that our dreams do matter, and in the end, they will define our lives; therefore, we in the dreamer's life know that if your dreams do not scare the hell out of you, then the dream will never be big enough to want to make into a lifestyle worth living.

We in the dreamer's life can see a world within a world, a hope for a better life, faith that it will be so, and the enthusiastic desire to place action into making those dreams a reality. We find knowledge to aid us, friends to encourage and guide us, and the strength in our willpower to overcome any obstacle against us or anything negative thrown at us to become that which we desire to see in ourselves as well as in others we wish to influence.

We also know that our dreams will expand as we find like-minded individuals whose dreams match or exceed our own, therefore giving our dreams a voice to be heard throughout the world.

Dreams are the window of the future and could be the foundation of the life you would like to build for yourself; they are the base of your heart, for if you do not wake up to your dreams every day, then you will eventually wake up to your nightmares.

These dreams that scare the hell out of you should become visions in your head that will never allow you to sleep; they should become so emotional that the desire for success is greater than the desire to quit.

> Your dream has to be so big, so emotional, and so
> filled with desire that your heart aches with each
> day that it is not yet fulfilled.

An emotional desire is a dream that does nothing more than inspire you to fulfill that dream.

From these emotional desires, you find inspiration enough to create a detailed vision; therefore, if your emotional dream does not become your inspiration for change, then your nightmares will forever haunt you.

No matter how big or how small your dream is, just dream; make it emotional, allow it to scare you, and more importantly, give thought to that dream.

How will you know that your dream becomes emotional? Let me enlighten you.

When your dream becomes emotional, you become so passionate about fulfilling it that you see nothing else; you envision yourself accomplishing that dream no matter the situations that will eventually arise, knowing that your frustration will be the emotion that fuels the fight to keep that dream alive in your heart as you make it a reality.

However, most people never seek out where to go next after finding that emotional dream. Well, here is my little secret.

> Whatever consumes your mind will eventually
> control your body.

Here in this book, we will look at diverse ways to learn to keep the dream alive; I will teach you how to keep it in your heart light to bring the dream you seek, whatever that dream may be, to life.

Step 1: Find Your Emotional Dream

- What are your dreams? Are they deep enough to make your heart ache?
- What is your why? Why do you want your dream to become a reality so badly?
- What sets fire to your soul? How badly do you desire to fulfill your dream?

READERS NOTES

Chapter 2

VISION

As you seek that emotional dream, keep in mind that if it does not scare the hell out of you, then it is not worth pursuing; it means the dream is not big enough.

Dream big, allowing it to scare you; know that fear is a different form of excitement, and to succeed, you must recognize, acknowledge, and remember that.

Now once you have that emotional dream that sets fire to your soul, the dream that gets you so excited that you cannot contain it, the dream that consumes your mind and places an eerie strength of desire to fulfill it—this is when you should write it down.

Give this dream detail, every word, every thought; this is creating a vision. Get a notebook, and write it all down; if you were living this dream in this moment, what would it look like? How would it feel? What would you see or do? What do you smell and hear? Utilize all your senses while writing the dream out.

Capitalize on those five senses; if you must, then even draw/paint a picture. Anything to put the fight in full view. Draw on that strength of the dream, knowing that the deeper you dig, the greater the dream becomes. And the greater your dream becomes, so you too shall follow to be great.

By writing down the details, large and small, you are representing the heart of your dream, therefore customizing your life. Your dream is your life customized; how do you want your life to look? Do not allow someone else to tell you how your dream is supposed to look or feel; their dream is not your dream.

A dream is a vision that does not ever let you
sleep.

Writing down and elaborating on your dreams, down to every detail, assists in finding your deepest and darkest secrets that you did not even know you had.

Your dreams are the foundation of your life; they are who you want to be, what you see yourself as in present and future times, and what you want from the depth of your life. If you do not have a dream you are willing to fight for, your desired life will never begin.

What do you want your life to be…strength and fortitude to be built upon or weakened to fall into oblivion?

Find your most motivating dream and write it out daily; this is defining your whole life. Your dream is your why, so define your why. This is the purpose of creating your vision, to strengthen and define your why. Your most motivating dream must be the base of your heart screaming to be built upon to become the window of your future.

As you build your dream, make sure to be logical as well as excited at the same time; do not be afraid to write everything down no matter how silly it seems. Just allow it to flow onto the page. Make it big, make it clear, and allow it to scare the hell out of you; it is time to wake up and have a vision based on your deepest desirable dream.

As you dive deep into your dream, you will find insight and inspiration, and you gain fortitude and strength allowing yourself to lean forward and lean into different thoughts and actions you never thought possible in your life.

Creating a vision based on your deepest and strongest dream will help you harness your life, so stretch your capacity to dream, and continue to customize the guidelines you wish to achieve in your life. Writing the dream down daily assists in always keeping the dream alive and in full view.

Documenting the dream will ensure that you have a broad view of what you want to achieve in your life. It will also help turn your fear into excitement and raw willpower to keep fighting for that dream to become a reality as you expand on your dreams.

Just imagine the lifestyle you want to live, then find a way to go live it.

- Turn your dream into a vision by writing it down.
- Imagine yourself in the lifestyle you want to live.
- Remember that your dream is the foundation.
- Without the foundation, your desired life will never begin.

Step 2: Create a Detailed Vision

- How do you want your life to look in the future?
- What adventures do you long for?

READERS NOTES

Chapter 3

<hr>

GOAL

In the last chapter, we spoke about creating a vision for the foundation of your life by writing down your emotional dream. Now here in this chapter, we delve deep on how to turn that vision into a goal to start the architecture work for the foundation of the dream.

The definition of goal: the end toward which effort is directed, also known as aim.

So as you turn your emotional dream into the desired foundation you seek, you in turn make it a "burning desire," and in turn that "burning desire" becomes the art of goal.

The Art of Goal

"That which becomes the object of your ambition or aim for a desired result always needs effort in action put toward it." That emotional dream you have written down is the first step into the art of goal.

There is a difference between dreams and goals.

Dreams versus Goals

- Dreams inspire you. Goals change your life.
- Dreams do not require focus. Goals require focus and work. Dreams stretch your imagination. Goals stretch you.
- Dreams require constant thought. Goals are actions with deadlines. Dreams create pictures in your mind. Goals are time-based tracking.
- Dreams have free run and are never-ending. Goals help you decide where to go next.
- Dreams alone do not produce. Goals produce with action.
- Dreams are result based. Goals have a cost.
- Dreams are not realistic. Goals must be realistic.

Goals are long-term convictions set with faith and the belief that with arduous work, results will happen. Goals will help determine the direction of your life; they assist with our ability to think long-term.

Goals are visions in writing with a time frame attached to them. All goals need to have a plan with a time frame; plan the work, then work that plan. Here in this chapter is where you plan the work, always keeping the goal in mind.

First, you always keep the goal in mind. Second step is that you start working backward from that end until you get to where you need to begin, step by step, and as you go unravel it from end to beginning. Third, once you get to the beginning by unraveling it at each phase of the thought process, you break that into smaller goals.

Even the smallest dreams need to have goals, but only you can decide what your life is going to be like; therefore, you need to break those dreams into smaller dreams and goals.

Once you get to the beginning of where your dreams are, look at your tasks, and place them into categories. Which are important, and which are not? Compartmentalize, organize, act on writing them down, and most important of all have fun getting each task done.

This is after all your life, so why not act now and put a time frame on your dreams and what you want them to be? However, just remember that keeping the illusion of what you do want your lifestyle to be in front of you can and will increase the desire to fulfill it. The most important thing you can do for your life is plan it and make the choice for your future; the clearer the dream is, the clearer the goal needs to be.

As you complete one goal, make sure you have another goal ready to work toward. Preparing yourself properly will be a major assist in exactly what you want from your life.

However, do not get so busy planning your life that you postpone your dreams—meaning, be sincere about working on your goals.

Primarily, remember, your desire trumps everything. From there, put a date on your dreams, setting time frames at every level. Ask yourself, "What are the goals that pull you out of your comfort zone?"

Your destiny is a matter of choice, a choice only you can make. So never lose sight of what is important; go ahead and see the good before it starts, always remembering that there are never any short-cuts to the things you are enthusiastic about.

The Art of Goal Setting

1. Be true to yourself.
2. Make your goals specific to your dreams and the lifestyle you desire to live > Detail your target!
3. Set goals at every level.
4. Goals must be meaningful and specific.
5. Goals must become the targets of your life.
6. Set goals for daily, weekly, monthly, and yearly.
7. Write goals down: written goals attract physicality.
8. Always know what you want.
9. Goals help us to realize the difference between wisher syndrome and worker syndrome.
10. Do something; it does not matter where you start…just start.
11. Fight for both the larger goals and the smaller goals.
12. Keep your goals believable and honest.

Remember: desire without a plan will get you nowhere. Become your best asset by planning your life and acting on it, be hung up on your goals, and make that the vehicle to take you to your dreams, always keeping the big picture in your mind and sight.

Know the difference between a dream and fantasy; a fantasy does not have a clear-cut plan, while a dream does.

Know that a dream with a time limit becomes a goal. Clarity of goals will count for 80 percent of your success. There is a feeling of magic when you write clear-cut plans to make the dream into a reality.

If something or someone is not aligned with your goals, they are not worth pursuing, so ask yourself daily what it is you need to do daily to get your dreams made into goals so that you can fulfill them that much faster.

And most important of all, if you want to hit your goal and fulfill your dreams, you must go after it with everything you have inside you to do so.

Time is of the essence, utilize it well.

Step 3: Write Down Goals

- Believable and honest.
- Smaller goals lead to larger goals.
- Step by step, then unravel it.
- Start with the end in mind.
- Detailed, meaningful, and specific.
- Written goals attract physicality.

READERS NOTES

Chapter 4

GAME PLAN

Now that we have our goals written down, we must form a *game plan*. The art of game planning is taking your goals and forming steps to achieve those goals.

The best thing to do in this is to take your goal to game plan, generating ideas and then applying those ideas to find which ideas work the best.

Here, your thought process is your asset. You start by remembering your emotional goals and dreams, revisit your why, and the dream that drives you. Capitalize on the fresh feeling your dream should constantly provide to you. The power of your why (your dream) should always remain your driving force. Solidify the conviction your emotional dream brings. Do not ignore it; let it flow within your heart and fester in your mind's eye. Let it capture the very essence of your soul.

Once you have that surrounding you, it is time to make those goals a commitment. By doing so, you are tapping into a higher cause—your higher cause. So get excited about those goals and dreams, and take them to heart, no matter what others say. Be excited about your dreams and convert that excitement into sheer adrenaline and action to match.

Game planning helps you go into life with the intention to win. Keep in mind that you are the architect of your own life, and only you can customize your life the way you see it.

Therefore, you are personally responsible for the life you choose to create; you define your reality. That means you decide which way you want to go; you oversee you. So make a decision to claim your kingdom. The best thing to do is start. It doesn't matter where you start; it just matters that you do in fact start.

Once you decide to start, your emotional dream will guide you and pull you by making your dream emotional. It will become a strong desire, which in turn will become the inspiration for your internal motivation.

Here is how to activate your internal motivation:

1. Look at what you desperately want.
2. Look at where you are currently at.
3. What burns in your heart should ignite emotions that either make you angry, frustrated, sad, or even all three, making you fight for the changes you want in your life.
4. Keep that desire and fight in front of you somehow. Either photos or on a wall anywhere you can see it is where it needs to always remain.
5. Write out a clear mental picture of what exactly it is you want.
6. Bring out your sheer focus on that desire to get that vision accomplished.
7. Take charge of your life.

Before you know the details, you must figure out the fundamentals.

1. Beginnings matter.

- It does not matter where you start; it only matters that you do start.

- If you know and see your end results, the important thing is to just start and go in the direction of your dreams.

2. Nobody is perfect.

- Never judge the imperfections of others, and most importantly, never judge yourself based on your own imperfections.
- Open hearts receive an abundance in love.
- There are no bad people, simply good people who make bad decisions.
- Stop torturing yourself, and start chasing your dreams.
- Benchmark against your potential, not your past.
- Life is not about "finding" yourself; it is about creating yourself.

3. Everyone has an opinion.

- Just because someone gives you advice does not mean you should follow it.
- Never take advice from someone who is in a worse position than you.
- Your goal is not to dictate but to discover.
- The grass is greener on the side in which you wander.
- We as human beings are the most motivated; however, we are also the most confused.
- If you do not stand for something, then you are going to fall for anything and eventually end up with nothing.

4. We are never promised tomorrow.

- Develop a sense of urgency.
- What you do with your time determines how you will live your life.
- Your life will not change after one hour. But after one hour, you can decide to change your life.

- For your future to change, you must first change your here and now.
- Now will always be the opportune time.
- It is not about where you are now; it is not about where you came from; it only matters where you are going.
- Anything great develops over time, not overnight.
- You cannot expect instant results in anything you want to accomplish.
- Purpose needs intentionality; if you want anything in life, you need to go after it with intense focus.
- You can never build anything on cruise control. If you understand the reason behind your why, you will always find the what and the how.
- When you know and understand the why, the what and how will always make an impact.
- In order to excel, you must be willing to do things others are not willing to do.
- Have the audacity to create an amazing life by setting your standards high in all aspects of your life.

5. Leverage everything you can.

- Intentions are wonderful; however, without leveraging on work ethic and accountability, your intentions will lead you nowhere.
- If you want to get results you never had, then you must do the things you have never done before.
- Be more aware of where you start; the day you become aware is the day your destiny will guide you to success.
- Start strong and stay strong by being sincere about working on your goals.
- People tend to go in the direction of the desire that drives them, so be a dream builder, and remember it is what is inside you that counts.
- The dream determines the distance, so with the right game plan in place, the dream becomes a slow reality, and with

the dream making the person, the person eventually makes the dream.

So make a decision, be honest with yourself, and be honest about your goals and your dream.

The game plan helps us to find a way to open our "floodgates" for success, assisting us in our choice to change instead of being forced to change. In any case, change triggers new processes.

Game planning is advanced decision-making and part of that requires you to write down whatever changes to make or the changes you think you need to make. Also, writing out your journey step by step as it comes to your mind or across your path will entice you to keep moving forward, as well as assist you to separate yourself from the masses by becoming the vision of your potential. Every human has the potential to surpass their current existing potential that they are experiencing. There is no limit to your potential. Just be better today than you were yesterday.

By having a certain standard for yourself and keeping with that standard, change comes easily when the purpose of the change is the larger focus.

Create your own mission statement:

- Visualize your success.
- Program your success.
- Turn your dream into a movement.
- Define the need to achieve your dream.
- Self-talk—positive words to yourself make all the difference.
- Stay strong on your decision.
- Expand on what you can do.
- Create your culture of standards.
- Find what you stand for, and be unreasonable when it comes to fighting for what you stand for—all progress depends on the unreasonable person.
- The biggest enemy of success is impatience and greed.
- True wealth is about finding joy in the journey of pursuing your goals and dreams.

- Do not get so busy chasing the dollar bill that you forget to plan your life.
- Play on your strengths, and practice on your weaknesses.
- Do not dig in doubt what you sow in faith.
- It is the changes you make that sculpt your life.
- Ideas are only great if you have the courage to execute them. Execution is the key to any great idea.
- Do not make a decision based on your comfort level. When you think of comfort, look at the life you are currently living. Nothing is going to happen in your comfort zone.
- Something in your heart knows there is always better.
- Be intentional about all you do; make intentional choices.
- Be open to corrections; corrections from mentors will give better sight and guidance to fulfill the dream.

Sometimes doing the work is harder than thinking about doing the work, so here are some tips to assist in the thinking part.

Tips for the Game Plan

- Find the thing you love to do and would be happy doing it for the rest of your life.
- Find what you are made of: character over credentials.
- Find a way to overcome opposition and challenging situations.
- Make yourself "in demand" instead of "being in control."
- Use your character in action to set an example. A game plan will determine how you go about the action; the action of work ethic and accountability will set a standard for you and those you desire to impact.

Keep in mind that to change the fruit of the tree
you must first change the roots of that tree. The
best way to do that is to start at the seed.

The choices we make will affect the gravity of the life we choose to live; do not fall for fiction, and make your goals realistic enough to make a game plan to fulfill your dreams.

You are the foundation of your life; it is your life. You create that foundation. How strong you have that foundation is up to you.

Step 4: Create a Game Plan.

- Have the goal ready with the end in mind.
- Put steps in place to achieve those goals.
- For each step put a timeline on them.
- Be excited and realistic about planning your life.
- Become the vision of your never-ending potential.
- Set your standards high in every aspect of your life.
- Leverage everything you can.
- Be aware of where you start.
- Beginnings matter.
- Be open-minded and intentional.
- You are the foundation of your life.
- Track your progress.
- Never miss a chance to grow.

READERS NOTES

21

Chapter 5

ATTITUDE

There is a fine line between attitude and self-image.

Attitude: a settled way of thinking or feeling about someone or something, typically one that is reflected in a person's behavior.

Attitude is how we react to challenges we come across and behaviors we have toward others, while self-image is the attitude we have about ourselves.

Having a good attitude is a key instrument in building a strong character and self-image, all while giving you a big heart. True wealth comes from precious moments that we create, and the key to that kind of wealth is the positive attitude we create. So whatever comes from the heart reaches the heart. Your passion is a large part of that; passion comes from the heart, seeps into the soul, and affects the mind. Therefore, we must be wholehearted in everything we do. And along with being wholehearted, we must also be happy.

Happiness comes from the worth of your dream and the people you decide to share it with; remember that dream is what you desire for your peace of mind. Therefore, wholeheartedness should include being happy while also having a fighting spirit.

To be genuinely happy, we must find joy in everything we do, no matter how hard it may get. Every day, everything, and all the people you encounter, all these are blessings even if the situation is not ideal.

Think of it like this: Someone who is having a difficult day will sometimes take it out on you; that is on them. However, how you react to that is on you. You can either bite back or take it in and analyze it. Ask yourself why they took out their anger on you; they are having a difficult day, and they just need someone to talk to. These days, people get worked up about anything, and many times they do not have anyone to talk to. So analyze the situation, and then find a way to make them smile. It is not easy, but at the end of the situation, it will be worth it.

Now not everyone will accept this at that point. It would be best to just walk away, and keep in mind that sometimes you win some, and sometimes you lose some. That is natural and inevitable.

Many times, when you are happy, the world will follow suit. Being happy will bring more productivity. Happy = productive.

Your dream is a part of that; dreams open a world of possibilities you never even realized were there in front of you. However, know that having that dream and chasing it will automatically sanctify you as crazy in the eyes of those who doubt you.

People are going to say things that will get under your skin; if people are not talking bad about you, then it means you are not doing anything worth talking about. Most people have limiting beliefs, and therefore, doubt will instill itself into the hearts of men and women around the world. "Doubt has killed more dreams than failure ever will" (anonymous).

> The worst prejudice we have is that in which we
> have for ourselves.

In that, we must have unwavering faith that action not only creates wealth but also cures fear. Faith is a substance of invisible hope. We must believe in the unseen. Belief is the acceptance of knowing something exists even if it is unseen. Belief supersedes science.

Here is the thing about belief, whichever thought you choose to believe, whether positive or negative, can become engraved in your being as a belief.

For example, if you believe you can accomplish anything, you will be able to accomplish anything.

Therefore, to reap the benefits of positive beliefs, we must keep positive thoughts flowing. Your brain is so much more powerful than you think and what you think, you will eventually be able to achieve anything you think of.

Your attitude depends on your thoughts and emotions. How you act/react to situations and others is based on your emotions. Your emotions turn into thoughts that will inadvertently affect your attitude.

The way to perceive a positive attitude is to follow these steps:

- Figure out what you want in life, and go after it.
- Keep in mind that the things we think about the most are the things we value the most.
- Recognize your potential, and expand your potential.
- Remember that your past does not define you; it will only refine you. *Use your past to fuel your future.*
- You cannot allow your weakest moments to determine how your life should be lived!
- Do not be afraid of the struggle.
- Stop highlighting your failures, and start improving on them.
- Change takes real determination; however, resisting change can lead to doing the same thing repeatedly while expecting different results (aka insanity).
- Respect the current journey that you are on, even if it is a negative one. All journeys lead to a positive outcome given determination and work ethic no matter how hard that journey is. Work the negative journey into a positive one.
- The reason some people get stuck is because they do not have the right attitude.

- As you find your weaknesses, find a way to refocus them and turn them into strengths.
- There is no point in judging people in general, but learning from others will only benefit you. So never compare your weaknesses to other people's strengths.
- The only true failure is giving up. So never quit, never give up, and never back down.
- Celebrate your failures, and keep in mind your failures will help you grow.
- We learn by making mistakes, so make as many mistakes as you can.
- Judge the book by the content, not the cover.

As you pursue your dreams, you are going to come across challenges, obstacles, and adversities. The objective of this is to push through them; think of these times as an adventure; this will bring you joy and something to laugh at later down the road of your journey. So smile and laugh in the face of adversity.

Negative begets negative; positive begets positive.

Little negatives + positive attitude = big blessings.

For example, I am accident-prone and have many days when weird stuff happens to me, but instead of getting upset about having these things happen and being in these situations, I look at how crazy they are, and I laugh and smile. Even on days when the little negatives are entirely my fault, I keep pushing forward because at the end of the day, I find good things happening to me.

What is life without challenges? Yes, your life *will* be tested; a lot of times those challenges and problems are the ones we have created for ourselves. Here is something to think on: resilient people do not focus on the negative; they focus on a solution to the negative and a way to become better through them.

They see their "problems" as "blessings in disguise," therefore, turning those "problems" into sheer focus to accomplish their greatest victories.

There will also be pain that will sometimes associate itself with these challenges, problems, and adversities. Pain is what transforms you; how you take the transformation is up to you. You can either wallow in self-pity from the pain, or you can rise above it. Only you can decide which path to take.

Never be afraid of making mistakes along the way: they help us learn and grow.

Here are tips to evaluate and free yourself from the fear of making mistakes:

1. Realize mistakes are a natural part of everyone's lives. We all make mistakes, young and old, and every age in between.
2. Realize that mistakes help us learn and grow. So what lessons are you learning from the mistakes you make?
3. Know that failures and mistakes lead to success if you take ownership of the mistakes you make.

And here is a small tracking system to go with it; get yourself a good pen and notebook to assist in your tracking:

1. Write down any mistakes or failures you have found yourself making.
2. What was the consequence of that mistake? What came of it (good or bad)? Write it down.
3. Evaluate what went wrong for the mistake/failure to happen. Find the exact moment that it all started. Keep writing it down.
4. Change tactics on how to fix the mistakes/failures to ensure that they will not happen again. Find what works, and move forward with a solution. Yes, write that down too.
5. Keep in mind that insanity is doing the same thing over and over while expecting different results. Therefore, change must be brought forth.

Many times, the things that happen to us are out of our control; however, how we react is entirely within our control. It is the attitude we have toward the things out of our control that helps us to build, change, and grow.

The goal here is to become a positive thinker, not a problem thinker; the power of positive thought will bring out the best attitude and the willpower to find a solution to any adversity, therefore creating a solution-finding mindset.

Remember that simply wishing the problem away will never solve it.

Step 5: Attitude

- Negative begets negative. Positive begets positive.
- How you act/react to negative situations depends on your attitude.
- Your base of control consists of how you choose to use your negative and your positive.
- Believe in the unseen. Believing and keeping positive actions and work ethic will make the unseen seen.
- Evaluate and free yourself of fear.

Chapter 6

SELF-IMAGE

I n the last chapter, I touched on attitude. For this chapter, we will discuss self-image.

Self-image is the attitude you have toward yourself. The attitude you have for yourself determines the attitude you have for the world, its occupants, and the dreams you desire to fulfill.

There are many ways to build your self-image; however, beware of the creation of vanity. As there is a fine line between attitude and self-image, there is also a fine line between self-image and vanity.

The definition of *vanity* is excessive pride in or admiration of one's appearance or achievements.

The definition of *self-image* is the idea one has of one's abilities, appearance, and personality.

So you see, one's self-image could easily be turned into vanity. Too much self-image becomes vanity. One way to keep vanity at bay is to read books that will teach you how to remain humble, as well as surround yourself with people whom you trust to tell you when you are acting a fool.

Another way to keep humble is to keep quiet in a "brag match."

A "brag match," as you can guess, is a group of people speaking highly of themselves to others while attempting to prove they are better than what they are.

As in all other aspects of this book, you will come upon two kinds of self-image:

1. Positive
2. Negative

There are many diverse kinds of negative self-image. It all starts with how you perceive yourself; many of us have told ourselves that were not good enough in some way.

Examples:

- "I'm so fat / so ugly."
- "I'm not smart enough / good enough."
- "I can't."
- "I'm horrible at doing things."
- "I'm worthless."

If any of these things sound familiar to you, it is okay; most or all of us have said these things to ourselves while feeling the effects of these negatives.

In this chapter, we will discuss how positive and negative will affect your life. And I will touch base on how to turn the negatives into positives.

Through all of this, you must remember that negative begets negative, and positive begets positive. Meaning that when you speak negative, negative things will happen. And the same thing is true about speaking positive; speaking with positivity brings positive things to our lives.

However, just speaking of positive things alone will not create complete positive results. Thinking and speaking positive are just the first step; to follow this, you must make small positive choices, and those choices can make all the difference.

As for the small positive choices, there are so many, so where do we start? We must start somewhere, so let us begin here.

1. Know that you cannot build anything until you first build yourself.
2. Know that doubt has killed more dreams than fear ever will.
3. Stop feeling guilty about the things you are unable to change.
4. Remember that positive things never happen automatically; small positive choices mixed with organized action will eventually bring large positive changes.

So let us start the analyzing process on those four points we discussed above. As said above, remember that you cannot build anything until you first build yourself, and to do that, you must forgive yourself.

Forgive Yourself

Everyone makes mistakes. When you are unable to forgive yourself, the pain of regret becomes too much to bear. And the pain of regret can become much greater than the pain of discipline if you are not conscious about it.

The longer you go without forgiving yourself, the more fear you will create for yourself in your life. And when fear outweighs the excitement of the pursuit of your dream, it will be #gameover.

> Records of wrong against yourself will eventually
> destroy the potential of your future self."

Doubt kills more dreams than fear ever will. Doubt comes from many places like friends, family, acquaintances, and even people we do not know. But the majority of doubt we receive is the doubt we receive from ourselves.

To rid doubt from family and friends and others who drive doubt into our lives, you must, by all means, *never* allow anyone to tell you who you are or who you should be. But be respectful when saying it. Remember, nobody can put you down without your permission. The trick with that is to never compare yourself with someone else in any aspect of your life, goals, dreams, or self-image.

By comparing yourself to someone else, you automatically open the door to others to put you down.

Doubt from ourselves, however, can be more difficult to manage, which brings us to this: know that you cannot build anything until you first build yourself.

Start by having the guts to believe in yourself. If you are not willing to believe in yourself, how will you ever believe in others?

Where the mind goes, the person usually follows. So if your mind starts to think of dreadful things, your body will eventually sink into depression and vice versa, so the best thing to think of is positive things and actions that will take you to positive things.

Love yourself enough to speak kind words to yourself in the mirror and throughout your day. Assuring yourself with positive affirmations throughout your day will give you a burst of energy as well as help you keep calm and cool-headed.

Step 6: Self-Image

Wherever you feel most powerful in your thoughts is where you must go and stay. Find where those thoughts are; go toward them even though they may scare you.

1. Have faith in yourself.
2. Draw on your talents.
3. Compete with who you were yesterday.
4. Dress a notch up if that will help you boost your spirits.
5. Think positive.
6. Have good grooming.
7. Keep smiling even if you are sad or angry.
8. Annoy with happiness, and kill with kindness.

9. Find or make thinking exercises to keep a happy heart and a hopeful mind.
10. Change "the music of the mind" by learning to master one weakness at a time.
11. Find ways to separate emotions.
    a. Leave personal at the door before work.
    b. Leave work at the door before returning home.

Remember, self-talk undermines doubt, and adversity motivates a winner, so never leave yourself to chance. Find faith through your self-talk, and know that you are the only one who can change you. And when you discover who you are, you will truly be free!

READERS NOTES

Chapter 7

WORK ETHIC

Now that we have touched base on self-image, it is time to go into depth on work ethic.

Keep in mind that changing your thought process is harder than you think, and there is always a chance that your mind will sometimes wander back to those negative thoughts.

Throughout all of this, you must keep in mind that the past can never be changed, but if you are willing, you can always shape your future.

And the best way to cure all insecurities is to put action into your dreams, goals, and life. Find a way to use your past to fuel your future.

How this is done is to look back at where you were: assess the pros, cons, good, bad, and the ugly. No matter what your past looks like, there are always going to be lessons in your past. And if you are willing to learn from those lessons, your past will benefit your future in one way or another.

Below are some ideas on assessing things going wrong in your life and how to use them to your advantage:

1. Seek a memory that has made it to the failure list, a mistake that made life hard or a challenge that put you on a different path that you wanted to be on.

2. Write it no matter how bad it makes you feel or how bad the issue was. This consists of the memory itself, followed by the exact moment when it all went wrong. Write that failure down, word for word, memory after memory.
3. Assess it: pick it apart until you know what went wrong, and ask yourself these questions:
    a. What was the consequence of that action?
    b. What did learn from that experience?
    c. How do I keep this from happening again so I can move forward and learn from this?
    d. How did my contribution to the failure/problem/mistake make it the way it ended up?

Go ahead and write all of this down; the goal of work ethic is to do, review, approve, and repeat.

Disappointment is the gap between trying and failing, and there will be a lot of trying and failing, therefore bringing disappointment with it. Throughout this process, it will be three steps forward, two steps back thing. It is called struggle, but do not be afraid of the struggle. Without struggle, there is no success.

Doubting yourself by highlighting your failures and dwelling on them gives more power over your emotions, attitude, and physical abilities to function with the wrong mindset.

Below is a system that I have been following to accomplish my dreams. I call it the stretch system.

1. Do—put action to your game plan.
2. Fail—eventually you will fail; it is a part of life, everyone fails eventually, no matter who or what.
3. Sort—using the process above, sort out the good/bad, pros/cons.
4. Learn—figure out a way to either fix the problem or start over. It does not matter where you start; just start.
5. Rearrange—let us face it, some plans just do not work, hence the reason for rearrangement. Start with your prior-

ities, the things you need the most, and figure out how to bring them to life.

6.   Replan—once you rearrange, start replanning, and rewrite the steps on how you intend to act. Remember, action cures fear, but you also have to mix that with faith. Faith + action = motivation with little or no fear that leads to progress and success.

7.   Redo—action! It is all you can do. This is where your work ethic comes into play. When you find the plan not working, how will you react? Will you get up and try again until you succeed, or will you give up and quit? That choice is yours.

When faith is the foundation, your fear disappears.

—author unknown

Remember that every time you miss a goal, you grow; hence the reason we need to fail.

Everything that comes at you in your life is a test; how you react to that test is up to you. You can either whine about it, or you can put in the stretch system I have given you above to assist in growing further for the sake of your future.

We grow because of our challenges, problems, mistakes, and failures. The goal is to review your past successes, have faith in the process even though you don't understand it at the time, and know what stops you from gaining what you seek.

Throughout this process, remember that failure should be considered a filtration process, not just one failure but *every* failure, because to have success at anything in life, you must step on every failure and use them as stepping stones for your future self to rise. Failure in any experience will eventually lead to success with the right mindset, work ethic, and lessons learned from said failures.

Know that it doesn't ever get easier; you just get stronger. The way to your success is to make sure your actions follow your belief and value system. Remember your dream every step of the journey because without the dream, the journey cannot take place and nothing will happen. The dream powers the process. The dream should power your work ethic and put your emotions to work in your favor. The dream motivates you to act.

Your goal is to become better, and by making those mistakes, you will eventually start seeing the results. After all, experience is the best teacher.

In pursuit of your journey, know that your belief will be tested to the maximum. The goal is to stay faithful to yourself and your dreams, and stay excited about your dreams and the journey you take by continually pursuing it.

There are three kinds of work ethic:

1. Wishing work ethic—this work ethic is wishing and wanting something but not going after it and working for it.
2. Half-ass work ethic—this work ethic contains little work ethic or just enough work ethic to get by. Also known as survival mode.
3. All-in work ethic—This work ethic contains heart, soul, mind, body, and spirit, along with mindset and attitude. If you want it, you go after it. Desire and drive are everything if you want to achieve your dream.

So let's dive into these types of work ethics starting at the top with number 1, wishing work ethic. We all know that wishing work ethic is just that. A wish is based on the hope that a dream or something will "magically" happen.

This is what the wishing work ethic is all about; people these days are so accustomed to getting something for nothing, but what those people don't understand is that the "something for nothing" concept creates lazy people, and no masterpiece is ever created by a lazy artist.

The biggest mistake in this area is that people want the dream, but they don't want to take the risk and go for it. However, what they don't know is that by not taking the risk to go after what they want is the largest and most dangerous risk of all, because if you're not committed to your dreams and you're not willing to do anything to catch it, you're eventually going to end up hurting yourself in the long run by becoming your own problem later on down the road.

People will give excuses to cover up their laziness, and the most common phrase we say to ourselves is, "I don't have the time."

In my opinion, that excuse originates from the emotion of the fear that the dream will never become reality, thinking it's impossible. However, the word *impossible* is just a reason for someone not to try. If they only knew that everything is possible, but wishing workers accept defeat without even trying. So the point to this is to stop wishing that you had done something to make your life better; get off the couch, get out, and start doing something.

Moving onto the half-ass work ethic. We have people who put their dreams in second place, making this the largest reason why people cannot successfully fulfill their dreams.

Placing your dream in second place creates procrastination, so the basic need to fulfill it slowly dies like the embers of a fire. It also creates retention and lack of motivation while living in survival mode.

Most people who lack motivation just settle for average, which is a dangerous game to play if you want your life to change.

Let's face it, everyone wants to have control of their time and their money, but few are willing to do the work to gain that control. More often than not, people are more afraid of the results than they are of the action, which allows the fear of uncertainty destroy the potential of the beauty of the road ahead; therefore, in a certain sense, they play "whack-a-mole" with their lives.

Most of the people in this work ethic bracket/category tend to get attached to the results. not realizing that being ambitious and being curious are two different things.

Being curious is just an inquiry about something or someone. Remember the phrase "curiosity killed the cat?" Well, here in the dream-fulfilling world, it's called "curiosity creates a vision."

That's all well and great, but without ambition, the dream will be null and void. Ambition along with curiosity go hand in hand. Ambition fires up the curiosity, which empowers the vision to become fuller and more achievable. But even ambition needs a boost every once in a while, and like I said before, most people in this bracket get so attached to the result that they just date success. And if you are just dating success, you will eventually marry failure even if you have optimism.

However, optimism alone will never be enough; hard work must come with it. You cannot make millions on a minimum wage work ethic; big dreams shrink with little or no work ethic.

Thus saying, "If you quit, it just means that you never really wanted the dream to begin with."

> He who lives without discipline; will die without honor.
>
> —unknown

It is a matter of choice, not chance.

Now as we move on to the all-in work ethic, the most important bracket of all, you will find that it's all about the choice you do make and the action you take to make your life better, for the choices we make today will affect how we live life tomorrow.

It all starts with your personal standards, meaning that the personal standards you make for yourself will determine the course of your life.

It is important to have dreams and goals in life, but it is more important to put action to those dreams by utilizing your free time wisely. So what you do with your free time will be a determining factor in how you live your life. Go ahead and go all in, create your personal standards, and let the emotion of regret go.

In order to do that, you have to stretch yourself by placing higher standards on yourself and take action toward your goals and dreams. Also, be willing to change your life, as well as change your boss by finding a way to become your own source of strength. And the best way to do that is to make a decision and follow it through by backing it with action.

Know that by becoming your own source of strength, you will be able to accomplish anything, and if you put your mind to your dreams, those dreams could eventually release you from anything that holds you back. Add excitement to those dreams and actions, and that focus will be a driving force. Whatever you focus on, you will grow.

Success will take a lot of hard work. However, if you don't do the work, the information you receive is useless. Therefore, you must learn how to maximize everything you learn; this will maximize your potential as long as you keep making small positive changes. Also, success doesn't happen automatically; you have to be an action junkie.

Small commitments = big results. All you can do is take it one day at a time, and just make sure you start. The reality of your passion is evident in your attitude and work ethic, so if you decide to start small, allow yourself to grow, and don't stay small. Opportunity is defined by the hand that keeps a hold of the dream and the action behind it.

Remarkable things take time, energy, action, and passion; staying consistent and persistent in the trenches creates success, and with succession comes fulfillment. Ambition is a wonderful thing; however, ambition can be your worst enemy if you apply it in all the wrong places. Where you apply your ambition counts for everything, meaning that even when you don't feel like doing the proper work to secure your future is when you need to get it done the most and at any cost.

The one thing in common between those who succeed and those who fail is that they don't like doing the work; the difference between those two is that those who succeed are the ones who do the work anyway. There is no minimum on work ethic, and in this bracket, it is the extra mile that counts the most. Inconsistence should *never* be on the menu.

If you sit around and "wait" for the right time to start, you will always be sitting and waiting, so the goal is to make the right time here and now.

Live with the faith that action cures fear and creates wealth, know that discipline comes before skill, and no one can force you, except yourself, to be motivated to go for your dreams and goals.

You cannot let your weakest moment dictate how your life should be lived; find ways to keep yourself motivated and on the forward path.

Discipline in one area of your life will eventually shine in other areas of your life down the road. Winners make adjustments; losers make excuses. Nothing is easier than speaking the words, and nothing is harder than acting on the words you say. So whatever you do say, say it with action that resonates from your heart, mind, body, soul, and spirit.

Everyone knows that decision is power, so the goal is to form habits that will help you grow. It is how we spend our time that will either shrink or expand your dreams.

Let us talk about some things that are required to keep you motivated:

- Find motivation wherever your inspiration comes from. Hopefully, it comes from the emotion you keep as you pursue your dreams while on your journey. Your destiny is determined by the size of your dream plus the amount of work you put behind it; however, your destiny can always change.
- Your daily habits should match up with your dreams, goals, and aspirations. What is relevant to you is where you should be going. Make sure you crystalize your dream by putting the work ethic behind it.
- Remember that you're the foundation of your dreams, which means that if you really want something, you have to be the one who goes out to get it. We all have more potential than what we perform at, so if you don't figure out yourself, your growth will never come. The same thing goes for moving small stones before moving mountains; therefore, when you upgrade yourself, everything else around you also upgrades. So always take it one notch up. If you keep doing the same thing as last year, your future will never prosper.

- Constantly expand by shedding fear. Expansion is the process of growth; the process of growth requires you to jump out of your comfort zone. You cannot have personal momentum without change and discomfort. The old you will never get new results, so do things your mind is uncomfortable doing. Always have the desire to be better than you were yesterday, and you should be in competition with only your past self.

- Focus on a few changes at a time. If you are serious about your future, something in your present is going to have to change. Whatever you do, under no circumstances should you run from the change. Always embrace the change. Victory does not come without pain or sacrifice.

- Create motivation by creating a positive outlook. Start by making small, smart, and positive choices, getting the battle underway by choosing to begin, and remembering that throughout the journey, it takes time to see success. Realize that fire and passion are not enough, and when you are in the zone, you learn from everything as you grow.

- Motivation needs discipline of work ethic to succeed, which means a little bit of effort goes a long way, and by showing that discipline, you will find the determining factor as you seek out and accomplish your destiny. Embracing change will always be a part of this territory, so do not fight it; take change and embrace it with a happy heart. Whatever happens in the dark will eventually shine in the light.

- Become a solution finder. The best way to handle challenges is to become tough, not just physically, but in all aspects of your life and emotions.

The key to this is to systematically develop a thought process.

- What is the return of interest on your work ethic?
- What will your future look like if you accomplish a consistent work ethic on your journey?

- Know that you have to have radical thinking to have a radical life, which means when you develop this thought process, it must be of your own design, and it must be written down so that it's not forgotten.

This brings us to tracking your progress:

- Write down your daily, monthly, and yearly.
- Track at every step.
- Keep in mind the one bite at a time concept.
- You do not "go"; you "become" mentality.
- Decision is power.
- The mere act of measuring your productivity will assist you in your personal growth and momentum.
- Track your game plan. Everything in existence has a cause and effect.
- Track the choices you make in your daily routine.

For all remarkable things, there is a price to pay, so always strive to be better than you were yesterday. Remember, experiencing is not only living but learning as well. One way to figure this out is to learn your weaknesses and use them to your advantage.

- Success comes with stupidity.
- Making mistakes is a natural part of the process.
- If you do not learn from your mistakes, they will eventually become repeated weaknesses later on in your life.
- Pain is what transforms you.
- Get to the roots of your unhealthy habits.
- To have what you never had before, you have to do the things you have never done before.
- It will never be easy, but in the end, it will be worth it.
- Be willing to pay the price of commitment.
- All sacrifices will eventually lead to success as long as your commitment to your dreams and goals is backed up with action.

Step 7: Work Ethic

- Make sure your actions speak so loudly that no one can hear what you say.
- Never leave yourself to chance.
- Be willing to do whatever it takes and more to fulfill your dreams and find the journey that will take you to your desired life.
- It is your ability to discipline yourself that keeps the fire burning.
- The choices you make in your daily routine compound over time. Choices compounded create the amazing.
- Do things that are unnatural until they become natural.
- Let your actions control your emotions.
- The decisions we make can either make or break us; the choice is yours and yours alone to make.
- So look at the challenges, set up your goals, find what motivates you, and go after your dreams and desires by putting the work ethic behind them.

READERS NOTES

Chapter 8

CONSISTENCY = HABIT = RESULTS

Consistency comes primarily from your work ethic or lack thereof.

The art of consistency is doing one thing over and over again until it becomes a habit. However, when you do the wrong things consistently, you will not get anywhere.

Not too long ago, my mentors told me, "Insanity is doing the same things over and over again while expecting different results." But as I see this statement, I realize that that statement can be misleading for certain topics, so allow me to elaborate on this a little.

Yes, doing the same things over and over again while expecting different results can become the art of insanity, that is if you constantly have the wrong work ethic for your future.

Let us dig into this concept a little deeper here. Say that you want a dream so desperately that you are willing to do anything to get it, but you keep falling short of that dream due to consistently using the wrong work ethic and not making the proper changes to move forward. This is considered negative insanity. However, this insanity will never be a good thing.

Therefore, positive insanity is just the opposite; when you have that dream that is so big that it makes you furious enough that it's not fulfilled, you should be willing to do whatever it takes to get it fulfilled.

Results come from small actions compounded over time, and with the right kind of action, you will cure both your anxiety and your fear while work will cure your worry.

So basically, consistency creates habit, clearly showing that what you put in, you will eventually get back. So make a positive, conscious effort on your work ethic.

Some questions to ask yourself in every phase of this journey:

- Is what I'm doing getting me free time?
- Is what I'm doing in my daily life consistent and positive?
- Is what I'm doing in my free time getting me closer to what I want, or is it hindering my progress?

If it is hindering your progress, reevaluate the thing you are doing, and realign your actions to match the dream journey. Start by focusing on that journey.

1. What steps are you taking on your journey?
   a. Are they helping or hindering your progress?
   b. What steps should you be taking on your journey toward success?
   c. Is your path clear in your mind?
2. Manage your energy.
   a. Keep positive thoughts even though it is not easy.
   b. Pick one habit, and work on it continuously for seven days (after seven days of consistency, you should form a new habit).
   c. Habits are learned; therefore, they can also be unlearned.
   d. Something you do only once is not considered a habit.
   e. Take notice of the minute details; sometimes they can make or break you.

3. Manage your emotions.
   a. Remember, success is not just a physical thing but also a mental thing.
   b. Your mind is like a parachute: it only works when it's open.
   c. Write down thoughts of discouragement, and play positive to negative.
   d. Remember the depth of your conviction: How far would you go to fulfill your dreams? What would you do to fulfill your greatest desire? What would you do if you know you could not fail?
   e. Stand for what you believe in, no matter what others say.
   f. Reflect on your gaps, and learn to fill them in.
   g. Know that there are no quick solutions and no shortcuts.
   h. Encourage a positive outlook on yourself.
   i. Recognize your own potential, and expand on it.
   j. Remember that life is going to happen, so have patience with yourself as you grow with the tides.
   k. Action without knowledge will lead to frustration.
4. Manage your time.
   a. Put value to your time.
   b. Become wholehearted in everything you do.
   c. Set aside time limits for the things that will and will not help you. Time limits on tasks will keep you from burnout, frustration, and discouragement.
   d. Break down your time. When you break down your time and keep to those set times, it will build your consistency rate, which in time will breed habit.

Remember, work ethic + consistency = habits = results. So work ethic is doing the actual work, while consistency is doing the work over and over until it breeds habit, and as you develop the habit, results will become evident.

And as we move into the results, which is just you fulfilling any dream that you seek, you realize that with this wonderful result that you have fulfilled, you have the feeling of an exciting emotional high.

Bringing in results is allowing the dream to go from the head to the heart as long as you follow the steps mentioned here in this book. And as you allow that to happen, you will continue to thrive.

READERS NOTES

Chapter 9

THE ENDLESS
TRIANGLE

Once you master the attitude and consistency of your work ethic, you will eventually build the habit, and in turn, the results will be tremendous. At that moment, you will find yourself in an endless cycle of self-discovery and growth.

Now in this, you can either be your greatest ally or your own worst enemy.

The goal of this book is to assist you in building something beyond what you dream and becoming the architect of your own future.

This endless triangle comes with the territory of growth through self-discovery, which is found in the process in this book. Your self-discovery comes from your ability to push through tough times as well as the way you build your work ethic into consistency.

As you go through self-discovery, you will in turn boost your self-image. The more you boost your self-image, the more you realize that there is no potential you can't reach.

Growth comes from different levels of success that is only found through challenges and failures. So understand that you have to strive to pay the price for what you want to accomplish.

As you boost your self-image through self-discovery, you will find happiness, which will in turn inspire others to want to change, as well as will help them build themselves.

The Endless Triangle

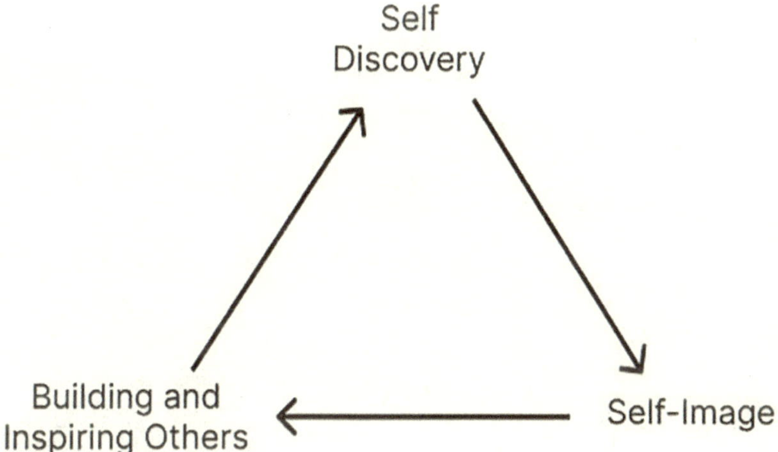

Chapter 10

RECAP

Now looking back at all of this, I hope you can see the future you desire.

Dreams are the hopes we keep in our hearts, the visions we hold in our minds, and the ache we have in our souls as we go about our lives. Dreams are the windows of the future and the foundation built by those who dare to dream a dream larger than themselves.

> Your dream has to be so big, so emotional, and so
> filled with desire that your heart aches with each
> day that it is not yet fulfilled.

An emotional desire is a dream that will not allow you to sleep and do nothing more than inspire you to fulfill it. If your emotional dream cannot inspire you, your nightmares will eventually haunt you.

Step 1: Find Your Emotional Dream

- What is your why?

- What are your dreams? Are they deep enough to make your heart ache?
- How much do you desire to see them fulfilled?
- What sets fire to your soul?

Once you have that emotional dream in your mind, take the time to write them down in full detail. Write out how it would look to be living that dream that you seek. Make sure you use every sense that you have to assist in the detail.

What would you be doing? Where would you go? What would you have, see, smell, and hear? What emotions would you feel?

The deeper you dig into that dream and the more you write it down, the greater it becomes, so how would you customize your life?

A dream is a vision that doesn't let you sleep.

Without a solid foundation, nothing else can be built. The vision is a blueprint of your life, so customize it to your standards by creating a vision that assists you in harnessing your why.

Step 2: Create a Detailed Vision

- How do you want to live your life?
- What adventures do you long for?

Goals are long-term convictions set with the faith and belief that you work to make them happen. Goals are dreams with time frames. Here is where we plan the work; the most important thing you can do with your life is plan it. So put a date on those dreams. The clearer the dream, the clearer the goal needs to be.

Set time frames at every level; if something is not aligned with your goals, then it's not worth pursuing and will need to be cut out of your life. Clarity of your goals counts for 80 percent of your success.

Step 3: Write Down Your Goals

- Make goals believable and honest.
- Smaller goals lead to larger goals.
- Step by step and unravel it.
- Detailed, meaningful, and specific.
- Written goals attract the physicality of the dream.

The art of game planning is taking your goals and forming steps to achieve them.

Generating ideas and applying them to see which ones work will assist you to capitalize on the fresh feelings your dreams provide and solidify the conviction they bring.

Tap into a higher cause by making a commitment; game planning helps you to go into life with the intention to win. You are the only one in charge of your life, so decide which way you want it to go. Activate your internal motivation; before you know the details, you have to know the fundamentals. Therefore, if you want the results you've never had, then you have to do the things you've never done before.

Game planning is advanced decision-making. By having a certain standard for yourself and keeping to that standard, change will eventually come easier as long as the purpose of change is the larger focus.

The choices we make will affect the gravity of the life we choose to live, so do not fall for fiction by creating a game plan that is unrealistic. Make sure your goals are realistic enough to make a game plan for them.

Step 4: Create a Game Plan

- Have a goal ready with the end in mind.
- Put steps in place to achieve those goals.
- For each step place a timeline on them.
- Be excited and realistic about planning your life.
- Become the vision of never-ending potential.

- Leverage everything you can.
- Be aware of where you start.
- Beginnings matter.
- Be open-minded and intentional about your goals.
- You are the foundation of your life.
- Track your progress.

Step 5: Attitude

Having a good attitude builds strong character and self-image.

The worst prejudice we have is that in which we
have against ourselves.

Keep the benefits of positive beliefs and positive thoughts by realizing that resilient people don't focus on the negative experience; they focus on a solution to the negative and a way to become better through it. Become a positive thinker, not a problem thinker.

The power of positive thought will bring out the best attitude and the willpower to find a solution to any problem, therefore creating a solution-oriented mindset. Simply wishing the problem away will never do.

Step 6: Self-Image

Self-image is the attitude you have about yourself, so find a way to be positive about you! However, remember that too much self-image can easily turn into vanity if it isn't nurtured properly. It helps to read book that keep you humble.

There are two kinds of self-image:

- Positive
- Negative

Negative begets negative, and positive begets positive.

Records of wrong against yourself will destroy
the potential of your future self.

Doubt kills more dreams than failure ever will; never allow anyone to tell you who you are or who you should be, and never underestimate yourself.

By comparing yourself to others, you automatically open the door for others to put you down. You cannot build anything until you first build yourself and that being where the mind goes, the person will typically follow.

Learn to separate work life from home life; learning to compartmentalize the different aspects of your life helps you focus. Wherever you feel most powerful is where you should be heading toward.

Self-talk undermines doubt, and adversity motivates a winner; you are the only one who can change you. Changing your thought process is harder than you think, and there is always a chance that your mind will wander back to negative thoughts.

Step 7: Work Ethic

Changing the past is impossible; however, if you are willing, you can shape your future by doing things differently in the here and now.

Disappointment is the gap between trying and failing; throughout the process, it will be a "three steps forward, two steps back" process. Just trust it. And do not be afraid of the struggle.

- Plan
- Do
- Fail
- Sort
- Learn
- Rearrange
- Replan
- Start again > action

When faith is your foundation, your fear disappears.

Every time you miss a goal, you grow. Everything that comes at you in life is a test, and how you react to that test is entirely up to you. Consider failure a filtration process, and keep in mind your dream, because your dream is what powers this process and it should motivate you to act.

Remember the three types of work ethic:

1. Wishing work ethic
2. Half-ass work ethic
3. All-in work ethic

Which one will you choose?

Step 8: Consistency = Habit = Results

Remarkable things take time and energy. Live with the faith that action creates wealth, discipline comes before skill, and no one can force you to be motivated enough to go for your dreams and goals except you.

If you're serious about your future, something in your present must change. Victory doesn't come without sacrifice. Motivation needs the discipline of work ethic to succeed. Whatever happens in the dark will eventually shine in the light, and decision is power.

Make sure your actions speak so loudly that people cannot hear what is being spoken. Never leave yourself to chance, and remember the choices you make in your daily life compound over time.

The art of consistency is doing one thing over and over until it becomes a habit. Know that it is a different feeling to fight for something worthwhile and that the right kind of consistency is executing on positive habits and work ethic. If you find something in your game plan that is hindering your progress, you should reevaluate the things you are doing.

- Manage your focus on the steps needed to take on your journey instead of the results.
- Manage your energy.
- Manage your emotions.
- Manage your time.

Consistency in a positive, proper work ethic will eventually breed habit. And once you master the attitude of the goals in this book, you will gain emotional enlightenment of self-discovery, which leads us to the endless triangle.

As you gain self-discovery, you will eventually boost your self-image, which in turn will eventually inspire others to want to change their lives for the better.

Remember, growth comes from different levels of success, and as people see your success, some will want to know how you changed, therefore inspiring them to take the chance on building themselves, thus once again boosting your self-discovery, starting the endless triangle all over again.

Anybody can succeed with the right work ethics; all you have to do is take charge of your life. However, expecting more of yourself and having heart in the game will help you master not only yourself but your dreams as well.

Consistency will lead to emotional and financial stability, and today's weakness will become tomorrow's strength. Life is going to happen; have patience with yourself as you grow. Know that your intensity is not as important as your consistency, so get a solid foot on your discipline.

In any industry, there is always a sacrifice. Price is what you pay; quality is what you get. However, action cures anxiety, and work cures worry. Stubbornness pays dividends when your heart is right, and only you can control the quitting part.

Remember that quiet desperation comes from a lack of fulfilling a dream, so what legacy do you want to leave behind? What destiny do you want to fulfill?

The choices we decide can either make us or break us; only you can be the designer of your own life. The determining factor is yours and yours alone to make. Choose wisely, and happy journeys, my friends.

ABOUT THE AUTHOR

J. J. Taylor (aka Jessica Taylor) was born in Salt Lake City, Utah, and raised in the surrounding areas of the Wasatch Mountains. In July 2016, She moved to Nashville, Tennessee, in pursuit of her dream of helping others through her writings. Throughout her life, J. J. Taylor has been writing a multitude of short stories and poems, which can be viewed on Vocal Media. For more great reads and more ranting and raving, you can find her poems and thoughts there.